Leopard Lady

# Leopard Lady

## A Life in Verse

Valerie Nieman

Press 53
*Winston-Salem*

Press 53, LLC
PO Box 30314
Winston-Salem, NC 27130

First Edition

Cover design by Kevin Morgan Watson

Cover art, "Leopard Lady," Copyright © 2013
by Valerie Nieman, used by permission of the artist.

Library of Congress Control Number
2018954710

Printed on acid-free paper
ISBN 978-1-941209-89-9

*For all who are on the threshold.*

The author thanks the editors of the publications in which these poems first appeared:

*Chautauqua,* "You Don't Leave It on the Side of the Road"

*Connotation Press: An Online Artifact,* "The Leopard Lady Finds Lost Things"

*The Heartland Review,* "The Gypsy"

*Heartwood,* "Sometimes Wishing"

*Hotel Worthy* (Press 53), "You Don't Leave It on the Side of the Road"

*The Missouri Review,* "I Take as Omens," "The Leopard Lady Tells Her Spots," "How I Was a Jig," "Blue Baby: The Professor Tells His Scar," "The Professor Lists Her Begats," "The Ballyhoo," "Like Mother"

*The Southern Poetry Review,* "The Leopard Lady Speaks"

*When Women Wake,* "'Marching Jay-bird'"

The author gratefully acknowledges support provided by grants from the North Carolina Arts Council and ArtsGreensboro, and the gift of contemplation offered by residencies at the Weymouth Center for the Arts and Humanities. A workshop experience at Coney Island USA, the Coney Island Museum, and Sideshows by the Seashore was critical in development of this book. Special thanks to Professor Marie Roberts, whose artistry and deep knowledge were inspirational.

Good readers are beyond price—Sarah Lindsay and Mark Smith-Soto and Kevin Rippin saw these poems as they arrived, and made them better. Thanks to friends near and far, with treats of jam and honey and encouragement when it was most needed, and Richard Bumgarner for timely gifts of books. Finally, thank you to my meticulous editor, Christopher Forrest, and to my publisher, Kevin Morgan Watson, for his constant support and enthusiasm for this work.

# Contents

*"It was not the show, it was the tale that you told."*
—Tom Norman, Showman

# The Leopard Lady Speaks

This leopard-skin come onto me
when I lost love,
(this is not for the marks to know)
when my man's absence
set a hot kindle of distrust
that blowed back on me
as lack of faith
in what is more worthy
than some handful of spit and dust.

No wonder I lost
my natural color, trying to be
all things to him, and him not wanting
what I ever was or become or any between—
turning away like a spoiled child,
turning away like the sun eat up
by the moon, and not my doing
or undoing.

I scourged my soul,
turning myself inside out
to make him a better tent
against the weather of the world,
stretching myself across his failings
like a worn-through quilt
on a wide cold bed.

They weren't enough left of me
to fill a thimble, then,
but I gathered myself back up
and stood, feet reasonable
to the earth, liver'n lights settling back
like I'd been dropped
from a high place,
and I was about satisfied,

but the letting-go of that man—
him of me then me of him—
left me streaked, specked, and spotted
like the flocks of Jacob,
and I opened my mouth to say
the true things that underprop the world.

# Book I: The Pitch

# Birth Day, 1935

I was born of a Wednesday
and full of woe, so they say.
My mother died in childbed and my father
seen only in that mirror I now hold up,
skin brown as a nut.
My red-haired mother died
before she could name me—a blessing,
someone said that, sure, a blessing.
Landlady took me out that rented room
where the ticking was sodden in blood
and gave me over to the Gastons,
grown old as Abraham n Sarah
waiting a child.
I gained a name and a sort of love
that kept me warm and fed
until scarce feathered, I fled.

## No More Haints

I heard an old woman so swear one afternoon
when I was working at the MacInernys, making sorghum.
The Gastons would send me out for wages,
*learning and earning* they said, and they leaned on the latter
once I had grammar enough to read the Good Book,
and a body strong enough for chopping and toting.

So come evening we let off hauling cane
and gave the mule his bucket. We was waiting
supper when the grandma let slip that haints
used to be about the place, a Yankee soldier
who had his leg took off in the parlor,
and a widow who walked and walked—
their souls bound to the house until the TVA
set poles down the road and run a wire for a light.
*They are made of fine stuff, and the crackle*
*outta that electric just pooft them away.*

The men laughed, but I kept that speaking close to my heart
and do believe it. The electric is made, I read in a magazine,
by pushing and pulling on the world's innards,
so in my wagon I have no part of such working.
I fill my oil lamps and trim them like I always done,
and I hang my pot over a fire outside.

No haints come to me, understand, not my mother,
nor the dead along the ruckus of the highway,
nor the souls sifting from whatever boneyard
we've neighbored for our camp, nor water spirits from those
drowned in rivers, nor ghostly mules that lead trapped men
out of collapsed coal mines to light and air.

The souls of all who breathe and those gone on before
are equal made of this fine material,
like spider thread hung with drops on a September dawn.
It can be plucked and it will hum.

# Call and Response

One day a man drove up
to take Old Sallie and three heifers.
In the back rode a man black as
the neathside of a shadow.

*What a colored girl doing way out here?*
he asked, looking me all up and down.
       I live here.
*What your name, missy?*
       Dinah. Dinah Gaston.
*You aint any Gaston child.*

The cows ruckused and fussed
til the driver hit one smart
on the nose, snapped his cane in half.
By and by the stock was loaded
on the truck.

*You work awful hard here, missy?*
       I do chores.
*Don't you got no people?*
       The Gastons.
*I'm meaning your own folk.*
       Preacher says I'm of the tribe of Ham.
*Chapter and verse, they sure can quote,*
*chapter and verse: "Cursed be Canaan;*
*a servant of servants."*

With the gate fastened up,
he set down, mopping his head,
and asked for water. I got him a dipper
and looked at his blue-black skin
and hair twisted gray.

       How come you're so black?
*Cause I'm colored like you.*
       Not like me.
*You might be a brownie, but you colored*
*all the same.*

*Now, you see that crow,*
*struttin through the corn?*
          Yessir.
*Ha. Well that crowbird, he's like us.*
          How?
*Black all on the outer, but open him up*
*and insides same as any of those white chickens.*
*But white folk think black*
*carry all the way through somehows. Scairt of it.*
          Why?
*Cause we're strong. Bodies strong,*
*spirit strong.*
          I'm right strong for my age.
*Missy, more'n you know.*
*How much blood it take to cast a pot of water red?*
          Not much.
*Colored blood powerful,*
*more'n any other blood.*
*One drop can turn a white man black,*
*make a woman a nigger wench*
*stead of a lady.*

# The Gypsy

First time I seen a fortune-teller
was the arcade at Traction Park,
the amusements hanging on
though the tracks was growed up
and the streetcar barns empty.
She weren't no God-made creature, but a creaking
thing of gears and canvas,
her booth pushed back
past the Skee-Balls. A nickel in a slot
sprung her to life, her gray head
lifting and her dead eyes lit with sparks
from the candle beside her.
A cape of old black stuff was wrapped
around her, dusty, but it rose and fell
on her stove-in chest.
Her hands was yellow as old candles
as they moved over the Mystic Tarot
*knows all tells all,*
then she palmed a card
that slid down,
five lucky numbers and a fortune.
The life gone outta her, then,
her hands still raised.
I stayed all the day in that dark hall,
spent the special nickels
the missionary church give us
to raise her four times.
Then I hung back and gathered up
the fortunes the others
tossed down, mocking,
but sometimes one
might look back,
feeling some kind of life in her.
Machine mayhap, but the Gypsy
chose a card for them
as she chose that last one for me:
*You understand what others only see.*

# Like Mother

*Aint it just like those kind*
*to be fertile as cats,* said the mister to the missus
in the parlor room of the house.

I know they was parlaying about me
and my belly, like I didn't know
how *that* come to pass.

The missus took me down to a root-worker
by the river. She had yarbs hanging
all over her shack, and one lamed-up old dog.

*Papooseroot,* she says. *It grows in the forest.*
*But you best know what all you're doing*
*or it'll kill ya both.*

She made up a bitters for me
from plants as grow in the deep woods,
lank things and dangerous.

*Drank this tonight,* she says, *and say*
*thow it away, thow it away, thow it away.*
*Blood will commence by and by.*

*Thow it away,* she tells me, *they be others.*
The next baby didn't stick around,
taking hisself off—just like I did right after,

putting my hopes like solid money
on the first kind face as come along,
figuring it better than that hillfarm.

Short but no way sweet, that companioning,
but long enough to spark a child. I counted my days
as the show headed down to winter quarters.

I asked and I found: a doctor in a dark office
that I come to through the back, and left the same,
bent over, creeping long the alleys.

Then once, it was in York State, I begged a tonic
from a woman as run a bawdy house, a work of night
and pulled shades, like blood gathered up in the body.

Well, I come to being solitary, and well satisfied
in that, til I met Shelby. And for love, for love, then
was no child to be made.

Fate in the lines on the side of my palm,
the children marked to me, *one two three four*:
what was tossed away not to be given again.

As for that first? I dreamt him many a night,
dreamt him standing by my cot, and he wore
a dent in his chin like the mister.

## Destroyed by Fire Flood and Ice

I leapt off the boxcar before the Oil City yard,
the man first down but not a hand
to help me over the clinkers.
Gallows-trees on the sidehills
and pump-jacks like to beat
dear life out of that knobbly ground—
no place I'd choose to set myself down.

We'd seen the lights, coming in, the Wheel
raring above the trees,
and the man says, *always work at a carny*,
though I figured more like he'd find
pockets unminded in the hurly-burly.

I was amazed first off
by a red tent painted over with gold hands:
Reader and Advisor Mrs. Elderia Ocean,
Gypsy Queen.
The man laughed at me, says, *Go on,
maybe she'll know your future.*

I recollected an arcade machine
sparked into life, but this old woman
was of flesh, rings on her fingers
and heavy jewels pulling at her ears.
Her voice was deep and creaky:
            *Do you dare to see the secrets past the veil?*
When she took my hand, seemed I was looking
at me through her eyes, then I was looking at her.
She spoke some foreign words,
run a crooked finger down my palm, bent my hand
into a cup, peered at me closely:

            *You come dressed as a boy
            but are woman born. You are with a man
            who is neither father nor husband.
            Cross my palm with silver
            and I will see the lover you seek.*

I got no coin to pay her,
so I turn her hand over
and tell out what I see:

>This town been destroyed by fire flood and ice,
>it is a place of dashed dreams.
>You are no gypsy but the wife of a farmer
>who et up your wealth like a pink hog.

When she spoke again, that deep sound was gone
and she wasn't no more than any other granny—
>*How did you learn this?*
I know it. In my head, I can see things.
>*Then why come to me?*
She set back, angry-like, and pulled her shawl
off her head. Her hair was thin and yellow.
Ma'am, I did not mean to rile you, by what I saw.
>*You think I am something to laugh at.*
>*Be on your way, and take your seeing with you.*

I slipped out the booth and the man was gone,
just like that. The midway emptied
whilst I stood there the longest, thinking,
well, he'll come back. The sound went away as the lights
went out, and just carny people ghosting
back and forth, most of em human-like.
I felt goose flesh
but it was just night falling cool, as twas September,
and farther north than ever I had been.

The old woman with her bent hands
come to pull her curtains for the night,
and she asked,
>*Child, where are you to go?*
No place, ma'am. I have no place to go.
>*Did he leave you then?*
Yes, ma'am. As you said, only sooner
than I expected.
>*Come in for the night. Aint much here*
>*but it's safe and warm.*

That is more than I have known,
and I thank you kindly.

I curled on the rug like a pup.
All night those pump-jacks went on
regular as heartbeats,
squalling metal on metal
like a rabbit's last cry.

# How I Was a Jig

I never danced til I step on that stage
in naught but a grass skirt and some beads—
the Gastons not holding with
card playing nor music
cept the shape-notes.

Straightaway as I hook on
with the traveling show,
this man (I learnt to call him The Patch)
come round asking if I wanted
*kindlier work than gen'ral labor—*
*like the sign says, no free rides.*
*We got a kootch show, and I got two*
*colored, plus you, as you're willing,*
*to make a jig show for the crackers.*

What is a jig, I asked.

*Why honey, you're a jig! Colored,*
*negro, jig. Jigaboo. You must come*
*from back of beyond*
*if you aint heard that by now.*
*Tell me you're eighteen, right?*
*Yeah, well, you aint gotta*
*do nothing but shimmy what you got.*

What I got, the other girls say,
warn't much.
You ought ta eat some fatback,
they tell me, put a little flesh on your bones.
Long's they see your titties, though,
it don't matter if they big.

So I jigged.
Made that grass skirt sing
like ripe wheat reaped
into the cradle, easy work long
as I did not look into the eyes
of the rubes, round and wet
as river stones.

The Patch says don't worry
when the inside talker
pulls the menfolk aside and speaks low,
*special drawing for one night—*
holding up a brass hotel key—
*you don't much get a chance*
*at a strong young girl like this,*
*firm as a new apple.*

It was what they call a con,
a key con, them red tickets
took up so careful,
one hope by one,
then throwed away to tumble
with the free wind
as we pulled stakes
and blew town.

# The Hunt

Times I was chastised
I lit out for the woods
to be shed of old missus Gaston and her switches.
Paths struck down to darklish pools
where spotted fish finned,
and cool mossy places
where I laid still as still,
aching from the rod not spared.

My feet found paths
pressed down by deer,
or some claimed Indian folk,
one about as rare as t'other in them days,
deer and turkey and all such creatures
been hunted out to put meat on the table.
Paths crossing to water and lacing
midst the laurel hells,
deer or red men moving light,
feet set in the selfsame places.
Paths like the trails cattle
cut along the sidehills.

*The lines of the hand are a map for the soul,*
Mrs. Elderia says.
*Not a prediction but a tendency.*
She takes my hands in her soft white ones.
*Earth you are, your hands square and practical.*
I tell her sure nough I grubbed dirt
til it was moreso part of me than what God
first scritched together.

She tells out my story:
*A life line long and deep, full of energy.*
*A heart line that starts between*
*the middle and index fingers, a sign*
*you fall in love easily, and here*
*it ends in heartache.*

She shakes her head.
      *Poor girl.*
Most like she's tipped that The Patch
has me warming his bed,
dues paid to be kootching and not
set down side of the road.
But that aint love nor neither is it heartache.
She looks at me close.
      *Now, if you want to learn*
      *to read palms then I will teach you,*
      *and you will have a skill of your own.*
That makes me drop my head cause
she has certain-sure seen it all in my lines.
      *I could use a helper, now, and you*
      *can be my legs til this mitt camp*
      *comes to you.*
I knowed the stink of sick on her from the first night
and now it catches like a bout of smoke
in the back of my throat.

      *Child, the hand you most use*
      *is what you make by taking hold of life.*
      *The other is your birthright. They start different*
      *and grow apart with the years.*
      *The hand shows earth, air, fire, or water*
      *by the shape of the palm and length of the fingers.*
      *The major lines are here, here, here and here—*
      *heart, head, life, and sometimes fate*
      *but sometimes not, and that person shapes*
      *his life all on his own.*

I asked her, do I have fate?
She stroked that line
right down, and I felt a chill go over me.

She showed me health, fame, money,
such as people ask most,
and said there were others to be learnt later,
Venus and Mars,
crosses and escapes.

*People think we tell fortunes*
*but what the palm offers is the soul,*
*how a person bears what life lays on us.*
Unless a body can see, I tell her.
*The first time I turned over your hand*
*I saw the Mystic Cross*
*and knew you had a talent.*
*So you can truly see?*
Sometimes.

———

Sometimes there is no seeing.
Like any gift it comes unexpected,
not to be grabbed after.

There is art, then, like Mrs. Elderia taught me,
how to read people first off by holding
their hands. Feel the damp palm,
how they almost pull away
from the touch of prophecy.
Then the tremble, the quickening pulse
when answers strike close.
In the dark tent, with flame holding
their eyes, you can see a mouth shrink
on a sour bit of news
or jowls go tight like a horse ready to spook.

Sometimes it's seeing, sometimes art.
And I learnt not to tell alls I see—
a word too much of truth, and the creature
trammeled close
is like to flee its bolthole.

———

Like the Hebrew children
marching through the Red Sea,
dry-shod where the hand of Jehovah
parted one side from the other,
still overspread with the terror
of the night, caught 'tween
fear and singing.

Like slaves hiding in the swamp,
following that drinking gourd north
along trails first trod by the Indians,
their ears pricked like deer.
Any sound could be a last.
Fill the babe's mouth
with a sugar tit soaked in pilfered brandy—
what is one more theft
when you are stealing yourself?
Swallow the cough, press the heart
from drumming bold enough to draw the chase.
Step down them narrow tracks
all the way to the wide Ohio,
a line of fate or heart or life, all three,
running twixt misery and hope.

The hand is a forest
cut through with paths.
Along them runs a soul
like deer to water.

# Seeing

The future can be seen
if through a veil darkly.

Few can see
but just as few

can see the past aright
any more than

they can spot
the air just out of their lungs.

## Waiting Seed

When it first come to me, this knowing,
it was like a bean seed busting clay crust with its back,
or more like jimsonweed or nightshade,
something untoward midst the crops been sowed.
I felt something rise up like a bubble
from the muck of a pond,
not to be stopped.

Now, I tell them what they want to hear, mostly.
*Is there money coming my way?*
*Does she love me true?*
*Why don't my son call from whar he is to ease my heart?*

This girl, soft as a willow in the wind, lets me
take her two hands and test the pulse in her thumb.
*How many children will I have?*
Her palms sweat.
You carry one now, I say, though you are no wedded wife.
She bobs her head. *I spect we will marry, soon enough.*
Something rises, fills my throat, and I see, I see it all.

The man is hatchet, fire, bullet. I see the curl of his lip.
The man is rope and bludgeon.
Not yet a killer, nary a word spoke against him,
but the seed is waiting to send down a black root
and spread poison leaves.
He will take a life. I see blood creep
into the clay, but not whose heart's opened.

When the road forks, I tell her,
depart quickly and take the lefthand path.
You must go alone.
Twill be rocky, no easy climb, but that way
lies long life. The lover's stroll longside the river
will lure you into quicksand.

She cocks her head. *But how many children?*
I see them rise up and blow away.
Three babes. Or none.
She pulls her hand from mine. *You are a cheat*
*and not to be believed, just like my Ronald said.*

# The Lot Manager

*We run a family show. I don't want to hear you wadded up some clem's cash in a scarf and stole it, telling em it's cursed, that sorta nonsense. You read palms and give em a fortune they can go home with happy. Their lives are hard enough.*

*Like I said, a family show. We got a reputation. Lions, Kiwanis, they all got us booked years out because we're clean. Mostly. Now, you do your dukkering act, like Mrs. Elderia taught you, and sell your lucky cards and trinkets, all right, but no funny stuff.*

Her banner laid on pallets,
her name struck out with white.
The sign painter holds his brush.

*Well, at least you're no gypsy. Them's trouble, now, always trouble. Mrs. Elderia, may she rest in peace, now she never give no trouble. Bohunk she was, or Polack. No ragheads on this lot, never been. Anyway, she spoke up good for you. If we was heading South then I wouldn't have a colored to run a joint, no siree, but up here you'll be right as rain. Watch your tongue. Find you an accent you can manage.*

*What you want on the banner? What's your moniker? Dinah? Won't go, it aint strong. We'll call you—what? Egyptian. They're dark people. Egyptian, yeah.*

The painter wants to know, *Egyptian what? Fortuneteller? Queen? Oracle? Sibyl?*

That one, I say. Sibyl.

## What I Could See


"Land of Eden" read the roadside marker
as we rolled in—sure a good omen, that this
was some soul's Eden, though hard to say why.

Leaksville Spray and Draper might make one town
altogether, but turned backs to one another like in-laws
on the outs, folding themselves around the cotton mills

that spew out men and girls, each and all
dusted white like snow come in summer.
*Lintheads*, the trick rider said, like one who knows.

That day the river run dark red under the bridges:
might be a slaughterhouse upstream,
but folk said it was just dye, no more'n that.

I shook it from my brain, then, arranging my joint,
crystal ball and cat skull, a turban on my pate
and a spangly shawl over my shoulders.

The show had a new ride jock,
name of Shelby, and he come gliding past my lot,
a strong yellow man with a quick smile, and all his hair.

Before we tore down, the town emptied of its jingle,
I made a marriage with Shelby, riding once around
on the Wheel. It was just after lot call, the grounds

clear of locals, and from up top we could see into Virginia
and that stretch of river running the tint of dungarees,
pouring into another river, the waters

side by each til past where we could see, blue an' brown,
and Shelby says to me, *We'll run on together like that, sweetie.*
Which was mostlike true, as we never blended

heart to heart and mind to mind same as we joined
bodies. One night he don't come back to our wagon,
though we never unturned that promise turn, never the Wheel

unwound. Now you ask how it is that I
couldn't foretell his leaving. Prophecy
is not a gift to line the pockets of the sighted,

but allowance to light the paths of others.
There was warnings enough in the broad daylight,
for any fool girl to see, and I would not.

And so I broke my heart
and the shoemaker's children go barefoot.

# I Could Take as Omens

I hear the owl bark
*hoo-hoo hoo-hoo hoooooo*
like a dog chained

and why when owl has wings
and eyes that it should
mourn I don't know

any more than night-passing
geese go baying
high up by the moon, hounds

on blood, a pack
digging its nails into the sky
and turning up stars.

# The Kangaroo Court Convenes

Lester swears he's dying
cause Ranny worked a root on him.
*Saw him myself at Beaufort,*
*conjure man in purple-tinted glasses.*
*They call him Doctor Buzzard.*

The judge demands, did you
put a curse on Lester?
*I don't know about no root.*
Her lazy tongue makes the words
another curse.

*She put it up under my wagon,*
*little pouch like a carrot.*
*I was scared of it so I burned it.*
Lester has naught to show but his own body,
eyes starting, flesh melting off in a way
that don't inspire confidence
in a Guess Your Weight man.

Ranny laughs.
Burying nor burning
won't end what is commenced in spite.
The debate begins, how to lift a curse with nary root,
nor worker, nor say-so of the one who bought it.
Finally, I speak up:
Holy water and prayer will kill the root.

I get my Bible and that little vial Mrs. Elderia
pressed last into my palm.
The whole tribe trails me to Lester's wagon,
where I sprinkle his doorstep and read out:
"As he loved cursing, so let it come unto him:
as he delighted not in blessing, so let it be far from him."
I dab my finger and draw on the door frame.
"As he clothed himself with cursing
like as with his garment, so let it come into his bowels
like water, and like oil into his bones."

25

That Ranny is a hard one—the Lord's words
make no nevermind to such.
She spits on the ground.
I finish off, "O GOD the Lord, for thy name's sake:
because thy mercy is good,
deliver thou" Lester.

The decision of the court is that Ranny
forever leave the show.
*Already gone*, she drawls,
*I got a Marine back there'll*
*keep me in shoes.* She switches
her busy ass away to pack her flimsies.

Lester looks like a poleaxed steer.

The sergeant-at-arms rattles the box,
relief fund fatter for our dimes and fines.
Oil poured on water,
the week's troubles settled, it's time
for japes and foolishness
til the stars stitch close our eyes.

## "Marching Jay-bird"

I once heard a banjo tune called by this name, a lively thing like a young soldier from wars long done, stepping off with buckles and buttons shining.

I well know the jay-bird, from north by the five lakes to Florida. He'll tattle the hunter and prowling cat, and run off buzzard and owl.

The jay-bird is most full of itself of any bird save the mocker, which is prideful for its talent, and the crow too has a good opinion of hisself.

My man Shelby was just such a one, his little belly stuck out afore him, and he would strut!

Jays are the only birds to call of a November morning when that wet chill comes down like the Last Day with Jesus on the doorstep.

Jay-birds creak and cry, never weary of their own name! Hoarders and reivers, I seen them snatch another bird's nest as a stashing place.

Acorn birds, so called, but they'll eat seeds or snakelings, hard bread, chicks in the nest, fairy-diddles in the piney woods.

This year past, acorns so deep even the squirrels let em be, heaps and windrows like skulls on the battlefield, and only the jay-birds marching to the harvest.

# Wealth

If I'd had money,
there'd been clean sheets on my bed ev'ry night.
Linen, with the scorch-smell of the iron on em
and a bolster to lean on
instead of that man.

# The Leopard Lady at the Market

I recollect it was Domino sugar
that missus Gaston had the mister bring home
for canning. She'd give him the ration cards
when he was burning gas to go to town,
and mind him what to buy.
But here I stand with two sacks of sugar,
one in each hand, and one weighs not a whit
more one than t'other. Matters not if the cover
be blue or white or poky-dots,
or what name is printed there.

Now I am half one thing half another
they say, but I am only one creature
in this world. My father's skin set me
out as a Negro, so called, but only half
of me harks to my father,
and I do not carry his name,
so why am I any more beholding
to him than to my mother,
who grew me up in her own body?

They say she was Irish, a folk
gifted with second sight,
that much and her red hair come true,
but the rest of her is folded
inside me, blood and bone.
She's working to get out, though,
showing herself.
That white woman what left me
is taking me back,
inch by inch.

First my hands spotted, as though someone
spattered bleach across em.
Then my elbows, knees,
like a map of some other world
set out in white like the best sugar.

If my mother takes me all
at last, til there's no shade of my father,
then what will I be?

# Given Name

When I was a jig I had no name
and no more room than to lay my body
down in the bunkhouse,
a narrow space as I was small
and come late to the show.

When I set to reading palms
I had a name I chose:
The Lady Sybil,
and a bigger bunk
where I kept my two books—the Bible
and *Tales from Shakespeare.*

I had men to give me names,
baby and sweetums and sugar,
but they was like side-o-the-road posies,
easy picked and easy dropped,
til Shelby, and he never called me but Dinah,
my given name,
and that mayhap was why I loved him.

When the spots showed on me,
I changed my name like my skin,
The Leopard Lady on stage,
Lady Panthera
in my own mitt camp.
Now I have names enough and space,
til I leave it all
and take the narrowest bunk.

# The Leopard Lady Finds Lost Things

Two farm boys shuffle outside my tent:
*Lady Panthera? You turn into a cat or sumpin?*
So the wicker chair crick-cracks. One sets an overbig hand
on the crystal; a streak of sweat shows and gone.

*It's my watch,* he says, *I lost it,* but he got another question
under his skin like a warble-grub about to burst.
Folk always asking after lost valuables to test and try me,
whilst their hearts pine after love or hope gone by.

He stares at the crystal as do they all, a place to rest
their eyes lessen they meet up with mine. This boy's fortune
is tied to the one outside, neither smart nor strong,
a weak pillar he could break had he more grit than girth.

Lost: someplace between sunrise and sunset, I tell him,
two golden hours, ev'ry minute a diamond.
It's a worthy saying I found in a brown book and squirreled
in my brain. No reward made for hours lost forever.

He lays his greenback dollar in the bowl.
*Well, it was a Timex. Seems like I'm paying you for nothing.*

Then come the word, as it come:

> Time secretly moves.
> Bends the alder branch.
> Seek under stone over sand.

His mouth gapes like a catfish, and I see
through his eyes the creek called Alder Branch,
a stone ledge by two paces of scuffled sand,
two bodies naked under the moon.

He will find the watch where he took it offen his wrist,
shudder at the question not asked.

# You Don't Leave It on the Side of the Road

Only the skunk
(who is precious in the sight
of the Almighty,
for His first-fingers marked its back
like you'd stroke a cat's)—

that piss-kitty
just humping across the road
headed for what egg-breaking
or cricket hunting
it does in the night—

when the tire finds it and the wheel,
(the bump too small to be a body
broken but it was), raises up
a smell from earth to heaven
like a mortal soul
clinched for the longest time
to the ankle of its death.

# Book II: The Reveal

## The Ballyhoo

Come up, come up ladies and gents, lads and lassies!
Rest your eyes on this glorious creature from Haiti's

floriferous mountains, the one and the only,
live and on stage, genuine Leopard Lady!

Abandoned by her lover, she called on black arts
of voodoo, summoning Erzulie of the heart,

unholy Mambo Madam of love and vengeance,
to trade her suffering for a beast's indifference.

By day our dappled Lady is as sweet as they come,
but beware the dreadful stroke of midnight! On some

nights when the moon blows white as a magnolia flower
and the wind is warm as breath, heavy with the power

of a tropical hurricane—now, it might be just such
a night as we have here, when the uncanny clutches

at our immortal souls—then, Mesdames, Messieurs,
she alters from frail woman into beast, conjured

complete with pointy fangs and claws and hairy pelt,
and, it's true, a twitching tail right where her svelte

bottom naturally ends! So come up, come closer
to see the Leopard Lady in the flesh, touch her

spots your very self, meet this strange mortal
suspended between the human and the animal.

Fear not, good folks, we keep the Leopard Lady secure
under lock and key once the show shuts down, to ensure

the safety of the public—especially those of the male
persuasion!—from her embrace, because fatal

that would prove. No cage needed for this sweetheart
of the isles: her bestial twin demands iron bars

and this massive Houdini-proof Master Lock
fastened on her door. So step on up, you can walk

right up and see her while she's tame, even hold
her magicked hand! Made just once and they broke the mold!

*And for the menfolk, a very special offer inside,*
*see what that silky scarlet kimono hides!*

## Arrivals

The selfsame day's we got the spotted cat,
this young fella come walking where the roustabouts
was driving stakes for the top
and all was a hurly-burly for setting the show.
A man grown, truth be told, but slender, his face
white as a book-page, and togged
from a High Street shop not the feed store.

He comes on smart,
following the banners going up on the line—
the lot manager puffing and a panting after him,
and I speculate
he might could be the law.
Instead we are gathered to hear
that this is our new inside man, Petey having left
us high and dry in Shinnston.

He tenders his hand manful like,
not flinching at the Snake Man's
scaly grip, taking my hand spotted as it is,
speaking just as equal to the Changeling and the Pinhead.
*My name's Jonathan.*
Don't matter none, everyone's thinking,
you'll be The Professor same's the others.

Directly, a stakebed truck pulls up
and they hoist up a cage—
a leopard for the menagerie.
They jostle the cage, poke the cat with sticks
until it snarls and leaps into its new box,
then commences to pace back and forth
and fix us with a yellow-eye stare.

*A spotted leopard, all tremor and flow and gaudy pelt,*
I hear him whisper, we both
having drawn close to see this beast.
It sends a chill over me.
        That is like out of a book, I say.
He turns to study me. *It comes from Dante.*
        I have some stories but not that one.
*I must tell it to you then.*

## The Professor: A Voice to Speak

When the narrow track that you've known all
your life tails off to boggy ground and weeds,
your feet will choose strange ways, and so I found
myself at the edge of town as darkness came down
and neon blinked and flashed on the carnival.
I asked after honest work, of a fireplug man
in striped pants like part of a uniform
he was caught abandoning. He didn't try
to conceal his mind—too young, too pale, too thin.
*Hey, Patch, we got that space in the grab joints yet?*
Not since Gus got him a queen, a voice
says from the tent.
                              *Now, you aint meant for rough
labor, that's a fact. So tell me what
makes you want to join the circus, son.*
I left school. I need to work and I have no ties.
*We got precious little call for book
learning. What can you do that's of use
to us?* I can—almost I uttered preach—
I know how to talk about things.
                              *So you can spiel?*
*Get a crowd together. Rouse em up?*
*Okay, gimme me a sample. Tell me how*
*Alfredo the Amazing Frog Boy came to be.*
I panicked—frogs?—all I knew was the plagues
of Egypt. But my homiletics class
had given me the gift to winnow out
ideas from the air with a sieve of words.

Folks, you know in the spring how the peeper frogs
sing til it seems they'd burst. Now, imagine that
times a hundred, times a thousand, day
and night, battalions of frogs singing high
as gnats, long-legged leapers of the field
braying in the middle, and great bullfrogs
making the sky vibrate with every whump.
These frogs were everywhere. In fields and streets,
on the rooftops, in the kneading troughs
and ovens. Not a plate set down, not a cup

poured that a frog was not inside. Between
the child and the breast. Between a man and wife
in their bed. Everywhere the frogs! Pharaoh's
land was poisoned, and still he would not let
the people go. You know it, chapter and verse.
The Bible is silent, though, about the babes
overshadowed in the womb by God's
decree. Egyptian children bore the taint
generation to generation, till you
today are privileged to see the last
of the line, for he has sworn there'll be no more
like him, twisted limbs and damp green skin
no more to terrify the land. So if
you're primed to set your eyes on a memorial
to God's great potency, then come inside.
Creatures beyond belief await your eyes!

Better'n George, allowed the voice from the tent.

*That's a talent you got, son. Lemme look*
*at you. Now, you're refined. I got some duds*
*that'll work for you just swell. Come back tomorrow.*
*I'll help you learn to pitch, long's you lay*
*off the Holy Joe material.*

## Blue Baby: The Professor Tells His Scar

All of us wear scars, it's true; some we
show and some we keep beneath our clothes.
It's only when the generator stops
chugging power through python cords
and the lot goes dark at the edge of some town
that I, button by button, open myself
to the night, as surgeons once cut and spread
my delicate ribs to find arteries
tangled around my heart.

Blue babies, they called us, but not for nursery
blankets and the boast of a boy. We were piped
wrong: our blood reversed its flow, got thick,
and skin and lips turned blue for lack of air.
I was three when my parents, despairing,
carried my limp self into the hospital
at Baltimore. Famous doctors undid
what God had done, made the blood whoosh back
into my lungs, and right away, they said,
I flushed pink, and lived.

The scar's so merged into my body now
that it's no shame any more, but as a child,
it was a constant reminder—born
without a heart, the other kids would say,
born without a heart and they had to put
one inside of me like Frankenstein.
My parents labored to explain: doctors
sewed up a hole, put a patch on my frayed heart,
stitched it all around like the sampler
that hung above my grandmother's bed—
*How sweet are thy words unto my taste! Yea,*
*sweeter than honey to my mouth!*

I asked her, what's a stitch, and she showed me
on that sampler—here is a feather stitch, satin
and cross stitch. Ladder, overcast, and star.
I chose the cross stitch, deciding that must be
the one, small silken crosses holding my
poor shivering heart together.

# The Professor Lists Her Begats

She is, as she tells me, a piece of work.
She is, as she tells me, a real catbird.
The Leopard Lady has lived a life these rubes
could not imagine.
               She tells me her *begats,*
as the first words of the Gospel count the sons
from Abraham to Jesus, not the daughters
whose dismissed bodies host the sons of men,
*and so the world on one leg goes crooked.*
It is a miracle play, of sorts, a tale
missing pieces, the places between filled
like the borders of a puzzle: here should be
trees, and there a cloudy patch of sky.

Born an orphan along the Ohio,
and drawn to water since—it may have been
some brothel where her mother died, the babe
alive in her pale arms had a skin too dark
for families who'd take a sunnier child.
Some sleight of hand before a sleepy judge
and presto-chango! she was Dinah, sent
to the childless Gastons for care—little of that,
as she was set to work as soon as her
small hands could wring a cloth or pull a weed.
Allowed a bit of schooling, she sought more
herself, reading the King James Bible, then books
she ferreted from trash cans and town dumps.
Shakespeare she loves, for stories *full o blood
and sorrow such as God allows Old Nick
to twist out of our souls.*

               Somehow, she gained
the Sight; accounts vary, maybe too keen
an edge to test, for I have heard three tales.
At fourteen, near as she could tell, she ran
off with a man who passed by one day on the road,
stopping to banter with her as she tilled and reaped.
She went in her feedsack dress and brogans, having
nothing to regret leaving. For the first time
in her life, she crossed over the county line.

But bumming was hard and money thin—she worked
and he stole, until she was abandoned, again,
in Pennsylvania, where Providence,
she says, had seen fit to set a carnival.
*They called me a forty-miler, not knowing*
*I'd already come a piece farther than that,*
she says, and not like to leave a place more kind
and work less hard than any she'd known.
*I was oft told, back on the farm, to stay*
*clear of gypsy folk and carneys or they*
*will steal you off, but I was already stole.*

She is, as she tells me, a piece of work.
She is, as she tells me, a real catbird.

# Devil's Work

Saints surely live each day
as it's provided and don't
test that yet-to-be,

but some of us the devil
sets to cribbing
the fence-rails of our flesh,

urges us to reach
blind-handed
into the next day,

put fingers in the toes
of unshook shoes
and roust the fiddleback,

put a heedless hand
under a rock. Most times naught
but dust or small bones

there, but once—the fright
of fingers thrust into
a coil of snakes

like zodiac wheeling
horoscopes round
about the world.

That's ever all the time
the serpent spake, but the gift rolled
like quicksilver in my heart

and never since been still.

# The Calling

I thought I heard the voice of God when I
was eight—a clear snap of something breaking,
a twig or bone, and in the space that was left,
my name. Jonathan. Oh, *Jonathan.*

Episcopalians, all, on my mother's side,
a glory of gold and lace and proper tales
of vocation. Noah walked with God, I learned,
and laggard Moses heard his name twice called.

In Sunday school and seminary, I
sought out the stories. I labored in the fields
of Aramaic, Hebrew, and Greek, as if
new letters would invite that voice again.

I did not ask for the earthquake nor the fire,
nor the great and mighty wind—only the still
small voice to once more say my name. Instead
it was *ma lekha po,* why are you here?

What had I to do with God? I walked
and waited, slept and sighed, dreamed for a dream,
but the lamp of God had long ago gone out,
and never again was my name called in the night.

# The Professor: "I Tremble to Meet Them"

It was no question of craft: the sword swallower
turned the bally and all his shows each day.
A sudden palsy, perhaps, or clench of throat—
he vomited blood, and died. Our painter brushed
chrome yellow across "The A-MAZ-ing Xerxes"
and red-lettered the name of his replacement.

The body, this bin of dust, can endure so much—
point and edge and heat and cold, nails thrust
into the nose, electricity on the skin.
The trick, I have learned, is that there is no trick—
talent must put a hand in the trap, disjoint
shoulders, eat glass, rest on the points of pins.

When I leave the show (and leave I will) the smells
will last me though I breathe dry leaves of books
each day thereafter. White gas on the fire
eater's torch—as much a taste on my tongue
as on his. Canvas. Body stench in the tent,
crowds pressing, dungarees stiff with corn dust,
pigshit, muck. The perfume the knife-thrower wears.

With our wagons circled at the back of the lot,
we hang our laundry, cook the food the rubes
have grown and harvested. A terrible life
to be bound to creatures and the soil. Nothing
to lift the weight of being from their backs.
No pledge, no turn, no prestige, nothing but
the cycle of toil, tethered like dumb oxen
on the threshing floor, treading eternal dirt.

They know no difference between the gaffs
and naturals, jostle equally
to see an illustrated man and world's
smallest girl. Made freaks maybe suit
the gawkers best—costumes and light and ink,
only an illusion. But the born freaks—
with fused fingers and ossified skin—
those are the dreams they shudder from, stare
then avert their eyes, imagine birthing.

The naturals are more dignified, despite
the warping God imposed upon their clay,
than the better part of His forsaken lambs.
The Snake Man smokes his briar pipe; Pinhead
holds no animus against the crowd.
The Monkey-Faced Girl lifts up her hymns of grace
while Insecta comforts the faceless sister who
lives inside her by stroking her perfect feet.
*It's Real!* screams the banner-line. *Alive!*

After the rumble of trains and lurch of horses,
the pounding and creaking and shrieking on the lot,
the unstable stage, then in the early quiet
I read Thoreau, lying on my bunk that smells
of a hundred particular towns, and not one:
". . . this matter to which I am bound has become
so strange to me. I fear not spirits, ghosts,
of which I am one—that my body might—
but I fear bodies, I tremble to meet them."

# The Leopard Lady Disputes with the Professor

The very instant he questioned me
about my seeing, I went for a sign.
I asked my Good Book, how do I answer him?
and leave the Bible open as it would.
My blind finger two times sought
and third time took up the passage:
"For they are a rebellious people, lying sons,
sons who will not hear
the instruction of the LORD,
who say to the seers, 'See not.'"

*Well now*, he says to me, *this is
a kind of divination by a book,
used by folk to tell the coming year
or the man a girl will marry.
But is it of God or of the deceiver?
For the Chosen People
are not to practice soothsaying,
nor to spell nor conjure,
"For all who do these things
are an abomination to the Lord."*

I read over the Bible near every night
and know a thing or three.
Such that Elisha told Joash to shoot out arrows
(*now that is belomancy*, he says)
and Gideon was give orders
to handle the fleece of a sheep,
and is there not Urim and Thummim
that Abraham asked, and Moses,
and David the little shepherd boy
what God made king?

*But those were in the Old Testament,
not the New,* (such folk have a sayback
for ever'thing, yet have not a discerning mind)
*for God spoke through the prophets
until the coming of Jesus.*

I know the Lord give us Light
that we mayn't stumble.
So says Micah:
"Night will come over you, without visions,
and darkness, without divination."

And by that speaking I silenced him.

# The Professor Tells Me of the Magdalene

She was in those times called bedeviled,
he tells me, but Mary was no harlot,
later men smirching her for fiery hair
and a speaking mind.

And that might be my mother,
who come to ill in that little river town,
fell into strange paths,
and died alone,
my birthing cry and her dying one
mingled as our breaths coming and going,
each of us on the verge of a new world
and most like to fall back
but we neither one did.

The Magdalene woman washed Jesus's feet
with the hair of her head,
kneeling down to wipe the dirt offen his toes,
and His feet not white
like on the pictures, but brown from the sun
and His toes broke from striking where He walked
here on the earth in his earthy form,
the cowsplats and stones and spit,

the Holy Land no sweeter
than any brown dirt what I hoed
or the black dirt or the red clay
that I have trod
on fields and fairgrounds
a sojourner always wherever I been.

# The Professor: Abracadabra

*Above all else, guard your heart, for it is the wellspring of life.*
—Proverbs 4:23

The half-man half-woman had just begun
John's turn to Jane when the tent began to spin
and I went sprawling on the trampled bark,
my heart flapping like a bird in my chest.
The crowd stayed back, sure that this was just
a part of the show, a carny trick to glean
their greasy quarters, but my folk, show folk,
lifted me up and carried me away,
laid me on my own narrow bed,
easing my shoes from my swollen feet, loosing
my tie, unbuttoning my scarlet vest,
my shirt. A spectacular turn, that scar,
but not a one drew back. Tetralogy
of Fallot, I said, and then, My heart. My heart.
I could have said Abracadabra,
but then all the lights went black.

---

White masks, and tang of alcohol. Who are
these men, their eyes and hands so cold, their mouths
concealed? *Mr. Wade, can you respond?*
Bright light in my eyes. *You're in the hospital,*
*you are safe now.* But how can I be safe
when my poor heart claws at the bars of my chest?
*Atrial arrhythmia. It's quite*
*common, a third of you tetralogy*
*cases. Has it been getting worse? Flutter?*
*Dizziness?* Yes, worse. Once I grabbed
a curtain, once sagged against the stage.
*Medication can help but is no cure.*
If God breaks the faithless heart to heal its woes,
is that his hand inside my chest?

They come visiting the ward in skewed
skirts and outdated suits. Our Pinhead sports
a slouch hat, failing to pass as rube. Fat Girl
and Alligator Man and King of the Dwarves—
the working acts can always walk among
the crowds unremarked, but naturals
are never off the stage, even here.
(Gawkers slow their steps and rudely stare
as my friends gather to hear my one true tale.)
Born blue, I explain, and my arteries
rerouted, but my heart will kick and dance,
the blood trying to find that old wrong road
around my heart. Their eyes are softer, now
that they have seen the scar. I am no more
the one who has the words, the Inside Man,
but one of them, stricken and marked.

I must take care, the doctors warn, my heart
is weak and the bitter quinine pills themselves
can make me faint. I lean on an ebony cane
that once I flourished, gloves no longer worn
for elegance but to hide the blood-red spots
stippling my hands and feet. My spotted friend
rests her hand by mine, photograph
and negative. *The white in me comes out
on my skin, but blood on yours,* she says, *a sign
that the God of Hosts bends close to those he wounds
and He will strengthen your heart, as much as your faith
will allow.* A constant singing in my ears
she claims are herald angels, but I hear cries.
Drowning cries.

## Fearfully, Wonderfully

I know you been speculating,
are them spots just painted on,
but you spy them for genuine as I go about
offering these souvenir cards—just ten cents
for the gents' amusement
and the ladies' instruction—
walking around so's you can see
this is my own veritable skin. Us folk,
here in the show, are a lesson
in the flesh; see, the blood of my body shows
through the white like it's paper.
Buy my card, just ten cents, gentlemen,
one thin dime.

In my days I been raised up
lowest to highest,
being now a natural,
as are called Show Nobility—
our world has top dog
and bottom, just like outside,
but honor's give not
for clink in the pocketbook
or fine name nor silk of hair.
After us who are shaped by God's thumb
come the working acts,
what have schooled their bodies
and borne up their hearts
in despite of suffering.
Those who semble savageness
or hatch their normal flesh
are just above those who show
gaffs—sorry sights
in pickle jars, misborne things,
and pelts pricked into new creatures.
Sometimes I ponder
if I aint such,
my skin a gaff—dark then light
like maps of faraway,
stretched cross these everyday bones.

I count my best money
from these pitch cards,
a picture of my spotted self
and a fine story: The change come on me
as a Sign from God,
*for she is fearfully and wonderfully made.*
Then a Bible verse:

*I will pass through all thy flock to day,*
*removing from thence all the speckled and spotted cattle,*
*and all the brown cattle among the sheep,*
*and the spotted and speckled among the goats:*
*and* of such *shall be my hire.*

But the fruitfulness of Jacob
is withheld from me,
and I ache like an old bruise that won't heal,
longing to be a mother
as I weren't mothered.

The gift of prophecy is a thin balm
for the stripes God's put on me
inside and out.

## The Professor: Fairy Stones

The Lady's a thin dime short for a hamburger
in the pie wagon, and so I pull the change
from my pocket. A cross among the coins.
*What's this*, the Lady asks, and holds it up.

A fairy stone, my Aunt Edwina found
it by a Virginia river, long ago.
*It's not a gaff?* She strokes its quartered arms
with nothing less than humble reverence.

It forms from molten rock, staurolite
(an explanation from the park brochure).
Aluminum, iron, and silica
snap to a grid, sixty or ninety degrees.

I recount the other tale, how woodland sprites
cried at the news of Jesus's death, their tears
freezing as crosses. That seems to satisfy
her neither more nor less than geology.

She wants this thing, I know, so why does my hand
curve for its return? The memory
of Edwina, wishing to be a priest herself?
A spark of what's dead, blowing back to life,

here in the show among the least of these?
I disgust myself. Scripture quick to mind,
or doggerel, *I Carry a Cross in My Pocket*,
recited by those secure in their salvation.

Was that what this is about, a speck of faith
not so much as the mustard seed, still here?
Or just the greed to save something of the past?
I'd gladly give Dinah every dime I have

in friendship, yet not this. I make a jest:
Hillfolk swear it wards away disease.
She drops it in my hand. *Then keep it close.*
I burn as I bury it among the silver.

# The Leopard Lady Tells Her Spots

Don't be looking
for what's daubed on that banner,
the Leopard Lady naked in the jungle,
brown skin all over with black spots
like wallpaper on a wall.

I'm moreso like a spotted hound
or the rump of the Apaloosey
our trick rider uses,
white strowed over dark,
but truly like the banner says
I am ALIVE!

Inside the tent
I rest on a high stool, wrapped
in red, til the Professor
brings them round and spiels a story
that aint mine.
I keep my back to the crowd
but they spy my hands, spotted
like troutfish, resting
on my shoulders. I hear them rustle
and breathe,
then I let the silk slide down.

*Nothing there,* one says out.
My back is perfect brown, cept
for a patch on my backbone just above
the spangly girdle I wear
for modesty but it's scarce that.
The silk be whispering louder
than them as the kimono falls
and I turn and stand.

They see me top to toe
allover speckled, face to breast to ankles,
my affliction being such that where
one side is marked
so will be t'other.

Here I am.

Then the light dims down,
the crowd shuffles along to see
the Terrible Snake Man of the Amazon,
and I gather up my red
to cover my nakedness.

# Highstriker

It was winter quarters
where I spied the newspaper at Giant's Camp,
a picture of four young men at a five-and-dime.
They wasn't supposed to sit at that counter.
They was *gonna* sit there, all day, ever'day,
til a black man could sit and drink a cup of coffee.
That's what they asked for,
a cup of coffee. And pie.

College boys, serious in glasses and overcoats,
they put me in mind of fellas
having a go at the highstriker.
The set of their mouths was like enough,
men gripping that maul and giving it
all they got, fixing to win a plush-toy for the lady,
but it was their eyes what said, we know this game is fixed.
Still, we're gonna try.

You understand how the highstriker's joed.
A front worker steps up, takes a lick,
mashes that lever so's all could see
the weight fly up to "he-man."
But when some stout farmer sets to the task,
the operator leans into a guy wire
and lets it go slack. No one's gonna ding that bell,
not a strong man among men, black nor white,
less the operator so decide.

Them students from North Carolina
are like a rube in some ragged town
who cottons on to how it works and sings out,
*He's got it rigged!*
and maybe The Patch comes and smooths things over.
The bell rings that night.
In that town.

Next time, I'm thinking,
next time stead of standing at the end
of some counter to collect my poke of food,
I might sit myself down.

# As Advertised (The Professor at the Park 'n Shop)

I heard the pop, knuckles to head, and saw
a boy leap back from where he'd tried to peek
beneath their skirts. He shook himself, a stunned
pup, and ran, howling, for his mother's side.
*They all do it,* Daisy said, *they try
to see how tis the two of us are joined together.*
(She and Violet now more alike
than in their show days—hair dye just the same,
their smocks the same, old woman's rouge
not greasepaint on their aging cheeks.)
Shoulder to shoulder, half turned away from one
another, the famous twins swung and swayed
as Daisy weighed the produce and Violet
put it deftly in the sack. *It sure gets old.*

I told her I was with the show and couldn't
pass through Charlotte without paying respects.
They smiled, the winsomeness that served them all
those years not yet disappeared. Onions
thumped into the bottom of the sack.
*Who's with your ten-in-one?* I named them off.
They'd crossed paths with Volta, the Rubber Man,
The Leopard Lady, and lonely Serpenta,
crawled home from a seven-week marriage
out in the world, which she found less than bliss.
A man is supposed to leave his mother's home
and cleave unto his wife, as the Hilton girls
cleave unto each other, but cleave also
means to part, which they could never do,
however they pined for some other union.

Descartes scissored body from soul, but can
they be untwined? Sisters twinned in more
than birth, joined in the womb, and where the blood
beats did the mind, nay, soul, not also touch?
Once a reporter asked them how they kept
their sanity. *We've come to peace,* they said,
*and learned to keep our spirits separate
though bound in body.*

We singletons, alone
in body and soul, endure each night without
the breath and weight of another form, without
an answering sigh in the dark. A different
sort of torment.

## The Professor's Suit

All the long day long, show folk are bought
and sold like candy floss to a thousand eyes—
late at night we regain our proper selves
and take up ordinary lives of soup
and dishes and darning socks.
                    But on this night
we were visited by wonders, a fall
of shooting stars. We let the fires die
and sat along the platform edge to see
the streaks of light, fireballs green and gold.
A show for us alone, and the whip-poor-wills
crying. The Skeleton Man sat with his love,
the Electric Girl, although he's pictured wed
to Lotta Mae, the quarter-ton sweetheart,
who chose instead to be the senior clown's
ample and vocal amour. And so it goes.

Dinah gasped and uttered little cries
at the celestial show, and I could not
help myself, I took her hand, and she
allowed me. Later, walking out along
the empty fields, cut hay sweetly stacked,
I took her hand again, and found my voice:
Dinah, I—
                    and she turned to hush my words.
*Dear Jonathan, do not.*
                    But I have—
*It's nowise fitting,* and I feared the words
to come: *You are like a son to me.*
Instead she said, *I also love you, but not
as the flesh hungers, moreso how Jesus spake
of greater love.*
                    *Agape,* I said,
the syllables far too bitter on my tongue.
It's from the Greek. Love for everyone—
*caritas* in Latin, so we say
faith and hope and charity.

                    The love
I scarred my knees to find, and broke the backs
of many weighty books without result.
*That is the word?*
                         It is one word, but many
kinds of love. I name them to myself—

Playful love or *ludus* that children have,
but my parents would not try another child,
and as for teenage flirtation, how could I
trust the heart that beat inside my chest?

*Eros* came once, a love I thought would kill
me dead, for the rider who joined the show midyear.
Powerful and dangerous as the horse
beneath her feet, and sharp with foreknowledge
of the fall that came quickly and brutally.

*Pragma* I will never know, the love
of those long married, rich with forbearance.
And as for self-love, most difficult of all—
to know the self, reflected as in a pool,
without falling for creation marred.

We stopped where the road made a T, painted signs
pointing to towns where people live with love,
or without. I told her our love was not *agape*,
but *philia*, between those who have endured
together, and known loss and sacrifice.

Then she reached for my hand, and held it tight.

## Another River Town

The show was on the lot and in the air
beside a river wide and dark
with the moon-boat sailing it
pretty as a picture-card,
but this town, now, turned its backside
to the water and hunched over its streets
like a dog on a raggedy bone.

I went round by the newspaper
tween midnight and morning
to learn the next day's word,
and found a big man amongst
the funnies and advertisements,
a black man shiny as the river, his eyes
yellow like that moon. It was good
to see a friendly face when most's
set against us show-folk
no matter what shade we be.

He set me a chair while we waited on the press,
and we talked, him laying out
why this strange weather,
the storms of wind and the floods.
*Spacemen*, he says.
Like from Mars?
*No, from us—our spacemen shot up there,*
*and when they hit on the moon*
*and planted they flag and all,*
*it got out of whack.*
*It's a balance, y'see—chords of gravity*
*gotta be tuned just right.*
He pulled out a quarter and set it on edge,
set it to spinning. *All you gotta do*, he said,
and leaned over and blew,
*and down she goes. Just a breath.*
*So them men on the moon*
*and machines a-running back and forth,*
*got it out of whack.*
*You can tell cause the signs aint right*
*no more. You know me, right, what I'm sayin?*

And I told him Yes, indeed, I knowed
the man of signs in the Almanac,
his skin pegged back
to scry the liver and the reins,
the heart and its meaning.
He told me how he timed his planting
to the moon and the zodiac,
*but my cucumbers curled like I planted them*
*in the sign of the toes, and it aint right.*

He limped away and I felt for him,
busted down in that misery place.
Then a bell rung out and the press cranked
like a night freight.
The papers come laddering up and he give me
one folded by his hands.
I stepped out to the loading dock
and the moon was running tiltways
down that river, the tight little town
not daring to watch.

# The Professor Considers Job's Tears

The lot was just coming to life when I took a stroll
among the booths the local gentry ran
to fund good works—displays of potted plants,
latticed pies I might have bought had not
"Job's Tears" caught my eye.
                              A woman thin
and bright as a needle told me the pearls, or so
they seemed, came from a weedy sort of corn
that produced these seeds *one on the other like*
*a steady flow of tears.*
                          The good man Job,
played upon by a casual God, as flies
to wanton boys indeed. And what answer
is he given for his manifold pains?
That God may not be known? Divinity
a wild force, whirlwinds gouging farmsteads from
their foursquare fields, the ceaseless sea that tears
ships in two and the land from itself. A God
who warps the flesh of the innocent in the womb,
and casts the flotsam up to breathe if they can,
eat how they must. How can a man compass
the workings of such, expect from the violence
some intelligible voice?
                          It's time
for me to take the stage. A rosary
for the Lady; though she's no Catholic, I know
she'll love the gleaming beads and the whittled cross.
*They're two-for,* the woman pitches, *all to aid*
*the good work of Our Lady of Mercy.* So
I choose a plain string of beads, no cross, and drop
it over my head and inside my none-too-clean
white shirt. Oh, we've grown close, Dinah and I,
image and negative, my stigmata
and her skin livid from the divine thumb.
Our Lady of Mercy, yes, who will not know
I silently share these living tears with her.

# Kentucky

Always told people my birthday come June 24. Appeared a good day to me, as I did not know my borning day for true. Midsummer Night, like that story in my book, all the folk bewitched and donkey-headed, and flowers liberal with their magic.

The Professor tells me I might need a certificate to show who I am, as though my flesh and breath weren't proof enough. He asked if I would do it *for him* and coughed a bit as he has a way of doing these days.

Anyways the show was passing through the county seat, which had grown none since I left, the courthouse still a hunkerdown pile of bricks with a porch on the front. We pushed through the big doors and right round to the Clerk.

Missus Gaston worked at the courthouse and I thought I'd see her there but I suppose she's dead these many years. It mighta been her sister though behind the high counter, the same sucked-in face as matched her soul, like an old dried apple forgot in a corner.

Dinah Gaston, I say, my name is Dinah Gaston and I was born in 19 and 35. I held my chin high so's her gaze didn't bust me down, a woman grown standing here not knowing her rightful day.

Old apple-face, she's proud, proper stuffed with having those big gray books to hand, floor to ceiling, full of people's lives. Don't matter none, cause my name is known to Jesus and writ in the Holy Book of Life.

She hauls down a book and goes to leafing through old yellow papers. *Baby girl born May 6 to unknown (deceased), adopted, given name Dinah family name Gaston, no middle name. Would you be wanting a copy of your certificate?*

Give me a funny feeling to ponder all those May 6s I passed unknowing, without even a shiver such as I would get stepping on my graveground. But now I have it, sealed.

# The Professor: She Brings Me Mayhaws

Crows were calling when I heard the knock
at my door.
              Summer, early, thin gray light,
and I'm listening to my heart beat beat beat.
*Are you about?* Dinah's gentle voice
rouses me to myself and I let her in.
*You seem peaked this morning.*
              Yes, I am
not up to lecturing, I fear. I'll have
to take tickets. She frowns (a comedown, to sit
on a stool while George stumbles through my spiel).

Then Dinah brightens like sun rising through clouds.
She lifts a Mason jar, a pint of clear
something—rosy, though, and thick. Not shine.
*Mayhaw jelly. I might could've made
it myself had I a kitchen and a place
to take up the haws, but our life don't so allow.
I let on to the advance man to keep an eye
along the road for a sign.*

              What are mayhaws?
*Berries, maybe closer to apples, that grow
by rivers. Handiest to come with boats
and scoop them from the water. Good for the heart,
strengthening. And tasty, Jonathan.*

She says my name softly, always, as though
there's some magic that might be startled free.
Seldom even among our own will she
say it, and never where outsiders put
their ears to the canvas, fascinated by us.

I hold her gift to the light, a pretty bit
of glass to refract the sun. These days they can
replace the heart, or use a machine to do
the beating for it. I hear these things but they
are as far away and alien as tales
I spin out for the locals. When I can.

I open the jar and find a spoon. Fragrant
and not too sweet—good indeed. I eat
two spoons while she watches, and nod my thanks.

Maybe it was the mayhaws, maybe Dinah's
care, but I was able to lecture that night.

## Sometimes Wishing

A mind will wander
hither and yon
when hands set to
some regular task—
here I am snipping
a peck of runner beans,
popping tails and tops
whilst the big pot comes
to a raring boil
and the greased spider
is smoking for corncake.

Woodsmoke and hot iron
I follow back
to Big Elk Branch
and missus Gaston teaching me
to put food by:
catsups and pickles and millionaire relish,
sweating at the Home Comfort
as we scalded peaches
in August and slipped them
from their bright skins,
stirring apple butter in the kettle
over a fire in the yard.
It was a labor
but afterwards a joy to see the jars
filled red and yellow
in that dirt-floor cellar,
a treasure-room
where women held the key.

Sometimes as we roll
past hayfields or tobacco
or cotton busting white
from the knife-edge bolls,
I recollect
the burn on my stooped back,
the itch of hay dust, the fiery sting
of the saddleback worm
whilst working the green corn,

but too the cold water trickling
over moss at the springhouse,
and birds flaring up
in the trees, and the mister's orchard
sweet both spring and fall.

I had nothing to call mine,
not even myself,
not like now when I have
my own place with my bits and pieces,
a box of books, a pot of chamomile
to take for my sleepless.
Still, I do pine at times
for the old place,
knowing that outside
the back door, mist is
lying in the arms of the hills
and the first wrenbird calling clear.

# The Professor Tells about the Wheel

Some say it's a wheel, he tells me,
this life we know, the soul
sent back again and again,
man become cat, monkey, a pine tree,
mayhap a beetle creeping
or a prince on a blood horse,
and no getting off til you learn
all that's needful on this earth.

I ponder wheels,
wagons and trucks and trains
rolling me hither and yon,
triple rings under the Big Top,
the Great Wheel,
Carousel, Roundup, Tilt-o-Whirl,

the Wall of Death
seems we all circle and circle,
but this Buddha said you could fly
free to a heaven place
not as we believe
(those folk lacking Jesus)
but close by Jehovah's throne.

I know my soul is sealed
and glory-bound,
but I would surely like
off this earthly wheel
of sadness.

*Attachment is the cause of pain,*
he says, and I hold his spotted hand
with mine and say, yes,
it is the wanting that makes the hurt
and not the having
nor even the losing.

# Gift

*Dinah,*
*open your hand.*

He puts that stony cross
on my palm
right where
the Mystic Cross
was marked at birth.

*It is yours.*

## See You Down the Road

### I. What We're Leaving Behind

It was early morning, blue cold,
when I come with the word:
Jonathan—the Professor—is dead.
They followed me, to gather round and peer
through the door to where I had left him
laid out on his bunk, peaceful
as though oversleeping,
someone having neglected to knock for him.

Someone recollected that a bird flew
under the top yestereve, portending a death.
I heard such when I was a little child,
the old people muttering *death* when a bird flew
into a window and fell stunned,
calling on Jesus when a sparrow come down
the chimney, thinking it a spirit sent to guide
a freed soul up through the blue.

The Patch come pushing through
with a doughnut still in his paw. *Poor luck
to have right now. Heart I guess.
Figgered that was coming. Poor luck to have here.*
Then he fixed me with his eye,
*Where are his people?
Where is he to be put to ground?*

I gave no answer,
for his passing weighed
on my heart, heavy as a wet stone.
Break of day, as was my wont
since he'd been poorly, I come around
to find him still under the covers.
*Help me get up*, he said.
I put my arms around him; many a time
I've propped him against the faints.
He leaned into me. I felt his body shudder
and when next I knew myself, I was clean across
the trailer, arms flung wide, pushed
by a great wind.
Jonathan rested still
and white as a china bowl on a shelf.
The spirit flown.

## II. Sparrows

It felt all of October, birds piping a single note
in the rain, no summer left in them.
Stripe-headed sparrows tumbled
cross the beat-down grass with the leaves,
common enough,
but one looked me straight in the eye.
I had 40 years on my back
and feeling every one of 80.

Long time ago, Jonathan let on where to reach
his family, so I fetched the scrap of paper
from the cigar box where I kept
my valuables, found a phone booth,
called and told them their fine son passed.

Before the undertaker come, we had our own funeral.
George, who spieled for Jonathan
when he was down, had a little brown Gideons,
worn at the edges, that he read from of a Sunday.
Testament and Psalms.
*In Luke it says, 'Are not five sparrows sold*
*for two farthings, and not one of them is forgotten*
*before God?'* He wet his lips.
*So we know our brother has gone to his reward.*
*There aint a sweeter soul in Heaven.*

And I stood forth then and said my say:
There's a special providence
in the fall of a sparrow.

The hearse pulled up and they commenced
to carrying him away.
*See you down the road*, we said,
one by one,
*See you down the road.*
I touched the door after it closed,
and spoke what we show folk never do,
Goodbye, Jonathan.

Then we blowed town, small creatures
that flock together
but now missing one
of our number, like to fall prey
to whatsoever waits along the road.

## Madame Dinah

"Let Me Live in a House
by the Side of the Road
and Be a Friend to Man."

A picture of a little white house
with smoke curling from the chimney,
them words beneath.
Long ago I tore it from a magazine
at the laundromat,
and kept it close where I laid down
my head each night—
always a place by the side of the road
but not long to tarry.

The Professor, he told me,
now you should get a place of your own
and be settled,
there's no life out on the road
any more. Come to find out
he had money tucked away
and left me the means.

So I have this house,
white, with square stones
going side by each to the door,
plenty of space with four rooms,
one for my readings
fitted up dark with velvet drapes.

My sign is raised up close by the road,
Madame Dinah, Palmist and Seer.
Every morning lights my gold hand,
and I remember Mrs. Elderia, her tent spotted
all over with little gold hands.

Now when it comes to friending man,
I have a truth laid upon me,
and the questions asked
I will answer
here by the side of the road.

# John 1:5

Prophesying aint hard
everything brings a word or two

leaves what blow inside
with the opening of a window

or door, turning up
curling into a letter

til the word rests on my forehead
like a cool hand on fever

storm times I am distracted
by wind in the trees

but rain come hammers
truth on the metal roof

# Ghost Riders (Coney Island Museum, 1980)

Once this all was Show—
til Dreamland burned, Luna Park burned,
Astroland, Steeplechase. Everything gone
but the Wonder Wheel, the Cyclone,
and the Parachute Jump lonely as one tree
left when a forest been laid to the axe.
All the electric past gone to ash
and smoke that thickens this sky.

I'm looking out an upstairs window
of Coney Island USA, like that aquarium
over there, a place set out for odd
and morphosized creatures
to breathe our different kind of air.
It's a comfort to rest here, among the banners
in red and yellow, the ride cars and costumes,
bits that's been saved.

Now it commences to rain. Hard rain, the gutters
pouring water. No one to ride up now
on the Wonder Wheel but the ghosts
of show folk taking their ease,
riding silent as kings
where no living bottom presses the plastic.

I see them all, Mrs. Elderia, Shelby,
advance men and talkers,
freaks banished from the banner line
as folk got so they weren't any more
willing to consider how unlikely
bodies was, even those
they lived in each day.
And The Professor. I see dear Jonathan in his fine togs
and top hat. He salutes me—even his ghostliness
is brighter than the others.

Down at the edge of the beach,
sand and salt keep gnawing
at the other. We are none of us more
than a handful of spit and dust.
We live and then we are melted into air.

# Notes

In "The Leopard Lady Finds Lost Things," she paraphrases a quote from Horace Mann: "Lost—yesterday, somewhere between sunrise and sunset, two golden hours, each set with sixty diamond minutes. No reward is offered, for they are gone forever."

The quotation in "The Professor: 'I Tremble to Meet Them'" is from Henry David Thoreau, "Ktaadn and the Maine Woods."

"As Advertised (The Professor at the Park 'n Shop)" draws on articles concerning the Hilton sisters, including "A Tale of Two Sisters" by David A. Moore in *Charlotte Magazine*. http://www.charlottemagazine.com/Charlotte-Magazine/July-2008/A-Tale-of-Two-Sisters/

Biblical quotations are drawn from The King James Bible.

The quotation in "Madame Dinah" is from "The House on the Side of the Road" by Sam Walter Foss, published in 1897. Public domain.

Valerie Nieman's latest book, *Leopard Lady: A Life in Verse*, joins two earlier collections from Press 53: *Wake Wake Wake* and *Hotel Worthy*. Her poems have appeared widely in journals and anthologies. She has held creative writing fellowships from the National Endowment for the Arts and the North Carolina Arts Council. A novel published by Press 53, *Blood Clay*, received the Eric Hoffer Award, and her fourth novel, *To the Bones*, will be published by West Virginia University Press. A graduate of West Virginia University and Queens University of Charlotte, she teaches writing at North Carolina A&T State University and at other venues including John C. Campbell Folk School. Visit Valerie's website at www.valnieman.com for news, book tour information, and samples of her work.

CPSIA information can be obtained
at www.ICGtesting.com
Printed in the USA
BVHW03s2126050918
526625BV00001B/14/P